Gentleman,
Single,
Refined
and
Selected
Poems

Gentleman,
Single, Refined
and
Selected Poems,
1937–1959

by
HJALMAR GULLBERG

Translated from the Swedish by
JUDITH MOFFETT

A Bilingual Edition

LOUISIANA STATE
UNIVERSITY PRESS
Baton Rouge and London

Translations copyright © 1979 by Judith Moffett. Original Swedish poems are reprinted here by permission of AB P.A. Norstedt & Söners Förlag, Stockholm, Sweden. Preface by Leif Sjöberg copyright © 1979 by Louisiana State University Press.

A number of the translations first appeared in *Modern Poetry in Translation*, *Translation*, *Music: The AGO and RCCO Magazine*, *Poet Lore*, and *Saxifrage*. "Balloons" first appeared in *New Yorker*; "Stellaria," "For the Demigods," "Delos, an Ode to the Young," and "A Lake There Is and Ever Nothing Then" appeared in *Poetry*.

Design: Dwight Agner
Typeface: VIP Electra
Composition: LSU Press
Printing: Thomson-Shore, Inc.
Binding: John H. Dekker & Son, Inc.

LIBRARY OF CONGRESS CATALOGING IN PUBLICATION DATA

Gullberg, Hjalmar Robert, 1898–1961.
   Gentleman, single, refined and selected poems, 1937–1959.
   Translation of Ensamstående bildad herre and other poems.
   Text of poems in English and Swedish.
   I. Moffett, Judith, 1942–   II. Title.
PT9875.G767A25   839.7′1′72   79–4596
ISBN 0–8071–0371–3

In memory of
CATHERINE DJURKLOU
*for many years executive secretary
of the Fulbright Commission in Sweden*

and to
KARIN LINTON,
her successor

Contents

Foreword

In the introductory poem of his first book, *I en främmande stad* (1927), Hjalmar Gullberg stated what for many years he would consider his mandate as a poet: *"att försvara det land som ingen har sett / och ingen skall se* ("to defend that land which no one has seen / and no one shall see"). Whereas Gautier defined himself as *"un homme pour qui le monde extérieur existe,"* Gullberg could be called a poet for whom the interior world exists, suggests Carl Fehrman in his book *Gullberg* (Stockholm: Norstedts, 1958). He adds that Gullberg more than once alluded to Jesus' assertion that "My kingdom is not of this world." It is, however, a matter of interpretation whether Gullberg should be considered an essentially Christian poet (Erik Hj. Linder) or a poet who at least employs Christian themes (Gunnar Brandell). In his book about Gullberg, Fehrman needed forty-five pages to explain the relationship of Gullberg the mystic to the Bhagavad-Gita, Thomas à Kempis, the *Tao tê Ching*, Meister Eckhart, etc. The poet himself stressed the individualism in his work and in an early interview suggested "Christian individualism" as a label, but this was to change drastically.

In his last, remarkable phase, comprising the collections *Deathmask and Eden* (1952), *Terzinas* (1958), and *Eyes, Lips* (1959)—most of which are to be found in Gullberg's *50 Poems* (1961)—the poet had dramatically altered the proportions of artfulness to matter in his poems and had abandoned the use of Christian myths:

> I believed in a god but he didn't know it,
> he was never to know that I went on believing in him
> even after he'd been dead for years.

Whatever may be left of these mythological characters is perhaps expressed in the poem "For the Demigods":

> If you've ever seen an octopus on a southern quay
> hurled upon the stone paving as though it had a dozen lives
> in every arm: the demigods are equally durable
> in a torture-chamber, at a place of execution—

xii/   their father's divine seed prolongs their suffering.
A dim memory of immortality
sits tight in the bloody mass. This explains why
it is often so arduous to flay them,
to disjoint and burn their flesh.

For you, these lilies, these stalks of hyssop
for you, this altar which is not an altar
in the ordinary sense but a staircase of song
            to the unendurable
            helpers at our need.

It may be useless to be categorical about Gullberg's religiosity. As Fehrman points out, shortly after Gullberg had denied his dependence on Christian mysticism he translated into Swedish Juan de la Cruz's work, the most glowing poetry of Spanish mysticism.

Judith Moffett not inappropriately opens her selections of Gullberg's poetry with his one sustained venture into the domain of comic verse, representing his fifth published book of poetry, *Ensamstående bildad herre* (Norstedts, Stockholm, 1935). The difficulties for a translator begin with the title. If "Gentleman, Single, Refined," sounds like the signature for a "personal" (marriage) advertisement, that's about right. But, then, whereas such ads were once common in Scandinavia, they are rarely seen in the United States. The alternative for the translator then becomes the footnote or commentary, which leads into scholarship rather than the re-creation of poetry! Moffett wisely restricted herself to including ten Örtstedt poems, and these are possibly the first comic verse of this kind to be translated successfully into English. (In a selection from Gullberg's first six books, *100 Poems* (1939), the poet himself was even stricter and included only eight).

In the space available I shall try to limit myself to observations about Moffett's translations and attempt a few brief hints to the uninitiated reader. Moffett's "the poor prof / 's head" (p. 3)—carrying the apostrophe by itself over to

the next line, might seem daring to the point of expedi-
ency, but is actually very much in line with Gullberg's own
practice in this particular work. In the first six books, at
least, he frequently uses allusions—to the Bible, the mys-
tics, mythological characters, to hymns, even to Goethe
and Shakespeare (*Julius Caesar*!); and in the title "Inled-
ning i frestelse" (p. 4) he echoes and reverses the Lord's
Prayer: "Lead us not into temptation, / but deliver us from
evil."

This professor found that language instruction and all
that it involves might occupy too much of his life. So he
employs an octopus to do the chores of marking papers
with eight hands, chosing his assistant from the same ani-
mal family as that of the *Nasobem* in Morgenstern's *Gal-
genlieder*. One difference in the two works is that the
emotional spectrum in Gullberg's text is wider than in
Morgenstern's.

By Moffett's choice of "Selected Poems, 1937–1959" a
concentration of the best of the later Gullberg has been
achieved. The first of those poems is "The Lake," in which
the poet demonstrates that he understands the unworldly
mystic Bernard of Clairvaux, as well as his squire. The con-
trast between them could hardly have been more marked:
the poet—often working with contrasts—indicates a need
to be a believer and a skeptic, simultaneously. But behind
it all is longing or some kind of expectation. *"Wenn Skep-
sis und Sehnsucht sich begatten, dann entsteht Mystik"*
(When skepticism and longing couple, then mysticism re-
sults), wrote Nietzsche; and this applies to Gullberg's kind
of religiosity. "The Lake" is an almost perfect example of
how a translation should appear.

In the next poem, "Proclamation in the Sea," Gullberg
has telescoped two kinds of prophecies: one utopian, from
the Old Testament ("They shall bend their sword into
plowshares, and their spears into pruning hooks; nation
shall not lift up sword against nation neither shall they
learn war any more," Eccles. II, 4), and the other, alleg-

xiv/ edly historical, about the Annunciation of the Blessed Virgin, and he has unified them "into a striking apocalyptic sea-vision" (Fehrman). The poem takes the Christian acronym ICHTHÝS, fish, and treats it as if the fish themselves, not just their name, were specially linked to Christ's name. According to Fehrman, the poem is Gullberg's "paradoxical answer to war propaganda and the arms-race." This is, incidentally, as close to a political statement as we will get in this selection. Gullberg wrote against the Nazis, but after the war he totally rejected his political poetry.

How much Gullberg's tone changes from his earlier phase is evident in the introductory poem of *Deathmask and Eden* (1952), "Singing Head." The poet makes no claim to be in league with the gods; he is no emissary, no saviour, no authority, not even a legendary Orpheus; he is a "singing head":

> Here, released from the weight of his limbs, from his belly
> and its accessory, the ultimate Orpheus comes:
> mutilated, blind, a chantey for seagulls
>   —only the washed
> face of a minstrel, only a mouth in its
> natural setting . . .

Apart from his interest in mysticism, Gullberg's orientation was languages. He had translated plays by Aristophanes, Euripides, and Sophocles, as well as Calderón and Lorca. He introduced Swedish readers to Sikelianós (to whom even Ekelöf dedicated one of his poems), and translated Gabriela Mistral, J. R. Jiménez, and Cavafy. Olle Holmberg recalls (*Hjalmar Gullberg*, 1966, p. 18) that the poet in later years said that the only place on earth which could inspire him with something resembling local patriotism or feeling for the home region was Place de l'Odeon in Paris! With this international orientation in mind, it is worth noticing a felicitiously translated poem, "In Lemnhult Churchyard," which reveals some local Swedish attachment. "A Lake There Is and Ever Nothing Then" contains much of the same eeriness as the Swedish original:

> A lake there is and ever nothing then,
> and the river is smoothed out in the gray mirror
> which no strand frames, no oar-strokes
> will ever crack. O ye blessedly averted ones, ye dead
> in self-sufficient beauty resting!

and, later on:

> Two vassal princes of a borderland—
> the pair of twins called Neither-Nor—command
> where the dog whimpers and the portals close.
> How man and woman differ no one knows
> with barrier on barrier undone:
> old and young,
>   beggarman, king,
>   equal one.

"Delos, an Ode to the Young" signals that the poet is heading away from the regions of Dionysus, toward the birthplace of Apollo—thus a return to the Apollonian approach:

> Experience—certainly, excellent! But
> him the gods love dies young.

Among other particularly well-translated poems should be mentioned the erotic poems "Stellaria," and especially "Snowbound," both narrative poems, and the final poems from *Eyes, Lips* (1959) when the poet was fey: for example "Written on the Poet's Birthday to Himself":

> What's best for man is never to be born.
> No stormy-petrel malcontent said this,
> no drunk *gourmand* with heartburn, feeling worn
>
> and sick, while settling up, for emphasis,
> before the hearse arrives for him and he's
> been hauled away. No, what I'm quoting is
>
> a well-known chorus speech from Sophocles. . . .

Also very fine are "Only One Wish," "I Dwell at a Resting-place," and the magnificent "Ballad," based on a Portuguese theme of great love:

xvi/

> Legends of love and death abound,
> we cannot count them all;
> but hers who out of graveyard mold
> was borne to palace hall
> has linked together love and death
> for aye in Portugal
>   The late belovéd Queen.

I would not be surprised if American readers of these Gullberg translations should ask: How is it Gullberg has not been translated more, and earlier? The answer is: because of the difficulties involved. W. H. Auden, on being shown some transliterations of Swedish rhymed poems (of which there are many), rather quickly decided this was going to be too complicated. "Even if I can rhyme, we'll get too far away from the originals, so what good is the rhyme?" he said. In the many translations Auden did from the Swedish all but a very few exceptions were free, unrhymed verse. Robert Bly has taken a similar attitude in translating Martinson, Ekelöf, and Tranströmer (in *Friends, You Drank Some Darkness*, Boston: Beacon Press, 1975). It should be added that Muriel Rukeyser has managed to complete Gunnar Ekelöf's book-length poem, *A Mölna Elegy* (published in *Comparative Criticism*, Spring, 1979), which in some sections requires rhymes and other intricacies, but her contribution has been unique in that regard. The rhythm and the rhyme have been the greatest stumbling block for would-be translators of Gullberg (and of a very substantial part of the best Swedish poetry). Most of those who have attempted to put these poems into rhymed verse have given up in despair. Moffett has had a rare persistence and has made good use of her considerable talents, and thus she has succeeded, by and large, very well; the matching of the unique Swedish vowel sounds can hardly be achieved in English.

That Judith Moffett has managed to persuade her publisher to include the original Swedish poems and has, successfully, translated Gullberg's rhymes speaks well for her, indeed. Who is she? Her poems have appeared in anthologies and magazines, among them *Poetry*, and in a respectable collection, *Keeping Time* (Louisiana State University Press, 1976). Her book is certainly not all rhymed and metrical poetry, but it does contain sonnets, villanelles, terza rima, a variety of received forms. It goes without saying that any poet who will try to tackle Gullberg will have to write formal poetry him/herself. From the very beginning Moffett responded to, and sought to imitate, the "formal" poets. Her first favorites were Kipling, Benét, and Vachel Lindsay. During her college years Auden, Yeats, and Frost were important to her. As a graduate student at the University of Wisconsin she had James Merrill as a teacher; ever since, Merrill has been a great influence on her, and she has completed a major study of Merrill's poetry. Her doctoral dissertation was on Stephen Vincent Benét and was directed by another poet of formal gifts, Daniel Hoffman. With those "elective affinities" and knowledge of Swedish from the time she was a Fulbright lecturer at the University of Lund (where Gullberg had begun his studies fifty years earlier), it was quite natural for her to take an interest in a poet who—apart from a few poems in Frederic Fleisher's *Seven Swedish poets* (1963)— had not been made available in English.

It is said that Hjalmar Gullberg occasionally "received" his poems ready and complete; but most, of course, went through different stages before they were finalized. The discipline Ms. Moffett has subjected herself to—and the ingenuity with which she has approached this project— has paid off. Whether she took more time than Gullberg himself in completing some of these poems is more than I know; but if she did, it would not surprise me. A more relevant question, however, is: are these poems well presented in English? My answer is definitely in the affirmative.

Leif Sjöberg

Acknowledgments

Work on these translations was made easier by the interest /xix and help of many people in Stockholm, Lund, and the United States. First thanks must go to the Fulbright Commission, the Swedish Institute, and the Nathhorst Foundation, whose combined generosity brought me to Sweden to work on this project and helped support me there for six months in 1973/74 and six more (in the case of the Swedish Institute) in 1976/77. Besides the four experts cited in the introduction, a number of people assisted me in official capacities: Olof Lagercrantz of the newspaper *Dagens nyheter*, Agneta Markås of Norstedts, Nils-Gustav Hildeman, Göran Huss, and John Walldén at the Swedish Institute, Karin Linton, Margareta Lindqvist, Birgitta Collin, and Antoinetta Oppenheimer from the Fulbright Commission, Leif Sjöberg of SUNY (Stony Brook), Daniel Hoffman, who was 1973/74 Consultant in Poetry at the Library of Congress, and Bertil Hökby and Arne Zettersten, respectively the Swedish cultural attachés in Washington and London in 1974.

My debt to the late Catherine Djurklou is measureless. For additional support—moral, material, and otherwise —I'm happy to thank Freddie and Hennie Bothén, Fred Fleisher, Muriel and Clas Larsson, Stig Olsson, John and Marge O'Shea, Per Rotander, and Countess Greta Thott, and also my parents. Much of the biographical and critical information in my introductory essay has been gratefully gleaned from Carl Fehrman's *Gullberg* and from Olle Holmberg's *Hjalmar Gullberg: en vänbok*.

These translations have received an award from the Translation Center at Columbia University, made possible by a grant from the National Endowment for the Arts.

Hjalmar Gullberg
and His Poetry

Hjalmar Gullberg was born in Malmö in southernmost Sweden on May 30, 1898, an illegitimate child. The father was a paper-company executive; the mother, susceptible to migraines and tending in later life toward paranoia and anxiety, may eventually have committed suicide. Gullberg grew up in the home of blue-collar foster parents whose name he adopted. The problematical circumstances of his parentage and birth seem to have marked him profoundly; for, however the facts combined to contradict his view of himself, he seems to have *felt* always alien, an outsider.

In point of fact, however, Gullberg could hardly have been more of an "establishment" figure. As a young man he was for years part of the intellectual community at the University of Lund. He earned there his *filosofie licentiat* (*fil. lic.*)—a degree roughly equivalent to an American Ph. D., although not then a terminal degree in Sweden and now no longer awarded—and in 1944 the university gave him an honorary doctorate. Between 1927 and 1961 he published ten volumes of poetry, the first six or seven of which won him a wide popular audience and the last three great critical respect. Some of his early lyrics, set to music, still are played over the Swedish radio now and then; virtually every Swede knows a song called "Kyssande vind" ("Kissing Wind") from his fourth book, *Love in the Twentieth Century*. He also produced several volumes of excellent translations from the classical and modern Greek and the Spanish.

Beginning in 1936, Gullberg was for fifteen years theatrical director of the national radio network, a position that made him an intimate of Sweden's best and best-known actors, writers, and directors of the thirties and forties. He was elected in 1940 to one of the eighteen chairs of membership on the Swedish Academy, the group responsible for selecting the winner of the Nobel Prize in Literature; and though the academy's deliberations are secret, Gullxxii/ berg is rumored to have several times personally pushed through the successful candidate. On top of everything else, he enjoyed a reputation as a Great Lover. Thanks to his radio and theater work, his academy membership, and the reception given his earlier lyrical poems, Gullberg in his forties had become a public poet in the manner of Vachel Lindsay, Carl Sandburg, Robert Frost, and Allen Ginsberg: in Sweden he was a sort of star.

Yet Hjalmar Gullberg was—on the evidence—a lonely and unhappy man, his student years in Lund and his final decade excepted. He was also plagued through much of his life by bad health. Countess Greta Thott, who met the poet around 1950 and stayed by him through his last difficult years, nursed him through several bouts of serious illness. Like his mother, Gullberg suffered from migraines; from the thirties onward he was susceptible to recurrent attacks of sciatica. Then in 1958, a day or two after his sixtieth birthday, he was found to have developed *myasthenia gravis*, a rare and usually terminal nerve disease. From February, 1959, until his death in the summer of 1961, Gullberg was in and out of hospitals; he was three times tracheotomized and placed in a respirator; three times the incision in his throat was sewn up again. When the disease was most severe he could neither swallow, nor cough, nor eat, nor talk, nor control a pen. His last book—incredibly, one of his two best—was entirely composed in the hospital, every line of it shakily scrawled down or dictated to Greta Thott despite the extreme pain and discomfort of the tracheotomy, when he was unable to speak at all, during the periods of his most desperate illness in the spring and summer of 1959.

In late 1960 and early 1961 the disease abated and the sufferer was released from the hospital. But a recurrence of symptoms began in June; and, rather than endure the torment of being tracheotomized again, Gullberg drowned himself in Lake Yddingen on July 19, 1961. One of his

most important poems, written years earlier—"A Lake   /xxiii
There Is and Ever Nothing Then"—suggests that the
drowning may have been a remedy planned and mentally
prepared long before the event, in case of need.

II CRITICAL SUMMARY

Just as Hjalmar Gullberg seems always to have felt a sense
of estrangement, despite popularity with readers and praise
from the Swedish literary elite, so does he always seem to
have been lonely despite his sexual conquests and a circle
of devoted lifelong friends. Personally as well as profes-
sionally, the facts seem to differ from his experience of
them. Moreover, his poems portray this solitariness not
merely as his private predicament but as a universal hu-
man condition.

Even taking the characteristic twentieth-century malaise
into account, there is something quintessentially Swedish
in this sense of isolatedness and also in Gullberg's concen-
tration on the elements of nature—sea, lake, bird, tree,
flower, grass—to the exclusion of personal relationships,
of love apart from its romantic conventions. The influen-
tial literary critic Olof Lagercrantz, in a controversial series
of articles appearing in the morning daily *Dagens Nyheter*
(August 19 and 21 and September 5, 1973), writes: "There
is a frightening loneliness about Gullberg. Society and his
fellow men do not exist in his work. His love poems can,
like the *Song of Solomon*, be interpreted as religious hymns.
There is no place for a partner." The last two books aside,
this assessment is fair. Gullberg's sensibility is for the ab-
stract; he addresses himself to religious questions, eternal
verities, philosophical proposals in their pure rather than
their applied forms. On so plain a poetic landscape the
relatively rare anecdotal poem ("The Lake," "Stellaria,"
"Balloons," "Ballad") comes as a relief.

The deepest-running force in Gullberg's poetry is reli-
gious, and its development, like that of Robert Lowell,

xxiv/ can be clearly traced in his work. Until the late age of fifty, and through seven volumes of verse, he was a conscious and farily orthodox Christian, his often quite lovely religious lyrics expressing—by means of unconventional imagery—essentially conventional beliefs ("The Lake," "Proclamation in the Sea," "The Lilies of the Field"). Then in 1952 his eighth book, *Deathmask and Eden*, broke a ten-year silence. Two poems in this book, "For the Demigods" and "I Believed in a God," voice a new antireligious position which shocked and disappointed many long-time Gullberg admirers. Some years afterward, in a newspaper interview (published in *Aftonbladet* on November 15, 1960), the poet stated categorically that he was no longer a Christian, giving as his reasons the many instances of mass suffering and killing—"wars, persecutions of the Jews, concentration camps"—occurring throughout world history and overwhelmingly in his own time.

Especially after the *myasthenia* struck him Gullberg wrote, instead of explicitly religious or antireligious poems, more and more about death—the final, hopeless visage of the religious impulse in his work. But the theme evolved through all its stages to the end without a falling-off of intensity; Gullberg was no less involved with religious issues after he lost his faith than while he still kept it. His 1932 poem "Rapture" (not included here) and "A Lake There Is and Ever Nothing Then" from 1952, two views of what awaits us after we die, make a chilling contrast; yet the same impulse produced them, and they belong together.

As a craftsman Gullberg never stopped developing. He had been from the first a remarkably clever and facile technician, but as a younger poet had displayed a weakness for striking poses and making choices for the sake of sound alone. His simple lyrical statements were often deftly and beautifully brought off, but as a group (though with important exceptions) they lack substance. But the landmark 1952 volume *Deathmask and Eden*, which signaled his reli-

gious turnabout, displayed equally radical formal changes.
It included Gullberg's first published verse structured by
neither rhyme nor scannable meter; and in it sense had at
last become more important than a lovely sound.

Many modern poets whose first work was written in re-
ceived forms have worked away from these forms in the
process of developing an individual voice. Unlike them,
Gullberg returned to rhyme and meter after *Deathmask
and Eden*, and when he did so it was to take formal con-
ventions more seriously than ever. After the invaluable
exercise of paying close attention in that book to what
words *mean*, he never again published an unsubstantial
lyric in the early style; but as a poet whose special gifts and
deepest instincts were lyrical, Gullberg would have dis-
carded his trump had he abandoned these forms perma-
nently. The title of his next volume, in fact, is *Terziner i
okonstens tid*—approximately, "tercets in a time not ap-
preciative of / conducive to art(fulness)." In this book ap-
pears a terza rima poem called "Snowbound"—together
with "A Lake There Is" one of the two most important
poems in the present selection, and in the *oeuvre*—which
his friend, the critic Olle Holmberg, rightly calls "Hjalmar
Gullberg's own Art poétique, directed against flab, spongi-
ness, a world in verse which froths at the mouth, form-
lessness, also injustice: the injustices of those things which
are formless against form."

The poems in terza rima and other lyric forms from this
volume are quite simply excellent; in my opinion, and that
of most critics, they comprise the best work of a thirty-five-
year practice. Despite a few troublesome idiosyncrasies
persisting to the last—involuted, tortured syntax, a preter-
natural fondness for rhetorical questions, inconsistencies
of tense—I'm convinced that had Hjalmar Gullberg been
born into a major language group, the ability to write such
poems would, or should, have made him an international
reputation.

III ABOUT PROFESSOR URTSTEDT

Half the twenty poems of *Gentleman, Single, Refined* (*Ensamstående bildad herre*)—Gullberg's single sustained venture into comedy—make up a third of the selections presented here. His Professor Urtstedt is modeled upon the antihero of Christian Morgenstern's *Galgenlieder* and its sequel *Palmström*, which he had read in the mid-twenties. Ridiculous and pathetic, funny and sad, the character projects Gullberg's version of surrealistic grotesquerie as Palmström projects Morgenstern's.

Professor Urtstedt—spelled Örtstedt in Swedish (*ört* means wort)—is no "professor" in the European sense. That, in the thirties, implied truly enormous dignity and prestige, neither of which poor Urtstedt possesses to any degree whatever. His is the looser, less jealous American usage. Urtstedt's title in Swedish is *läroverksadjunkt*, or simply *adjunkt*, and he teaches German in a secondary school called a *gymnasium*. But the Swedish and American public educational systems differed, and differ, in important ways; even in Urtstedt's day an *adjunkt* would have needed at least a *fil. mag.* (M.A.) degree. I've "translated" Urtstedt into the equivalent, more or less, of a teacher at a (perhaps not very prestigious) American college—not really a satisfactory solution, but I hope a workable one.

Urtstedt is a tragicomic figure: rather sweet—but skinny, shy, inept at friendship and romance, picked on or ignored by those around him. His sensitive nerves, his sensitive feelings, are forever being ridden over roughshod. He publishes a book of verse only to have it panned by a reviewer who is, to add insult to injury, a former student of his (this is the Tidström who appears here only in "Keeping the Sabbath," out for a Sunday drive with Urtstedt's neighbor and nemesis, Vikingson, and a couple of chorus girls). He also has terrible luck, and at the end of the book he dies, unnoticed and unmourned but for the brief attentions of an octopus trained to be his secretary.

Critics have sometimes viewed the book as an exercise /xxvii
in self-pity; Gullberg had after all himself been a teacher
in a *gymnasium* for a time, was himself a poet, and had
himself published a poem—"Proclamation in the Sea,"
originally entitled "Dream of Peace"—which suffered a
fate similar to that of Urtstedt's work by the same title (de-
scribed in a poem not included here). In no obvious ways
did the two otherwise resemble one another, but one may
consider whether Urtstedt's agonizing insecurity and iso-
lation don't reveal something about the poet's private self-
image. Holmberg puts the psychological truth succinctly:
"Hjalmar Gullberg was, when he wrote *Gentleman, Sin-
gle, Refined*, himself a well-fed, well-off, well-tailored gen-
tleman, and presumably the object of many wistful femi-
nine sighs. Had he—perchance—not become all that, he
might well have become an *adjunkt* Örtstedt."

IV A NOTE ON THE TRANSLATION

Frankly, translating in such a way that rhymes and rhythms go
into English hell or high water has proved to be such a disaster
in the past—it has been abandoned by almost all living transla-
tors—that I wouldn't recommend it to anyone. That way will
just result in a massacre. If the translator keeps rhyme and
rhythm, image and meaning will suffer, since you must lose
something. I don't think any poet, no matter how conservative,
wants to see his meaning and images mangled.
                    Robert Bly

The prevalence [in American translating] of a period style and
aesthetic has facilitated the wholesale Englishing of foreign poets,
with results which are often valuable but which might persuade
the unwary that Syrians and Chileans came out of the same
Midwestern workshop. . . . I believe that from my point of view
—that of one who says some of his say through the experimen-
tal use of "traditional forms"—the Russians are the world's best
translators. A friend has assured me that a translation of "After
the Last Bulletins," published in *Literaturnaya Gazeta*, is utterly
faithful and better than the original; and I have seen or heard of
other translations by Russians which went after whole poems of
mine, alliterations and all. I am grateful to translators who don't

xxviii/   water me down to free verse, and I try to reciprocate whenever I can. I've just given three weeks to doing a 48-line rhymed translation of a poem of Joseph Brodsky's, and could have given no less.

Richard Wilbur

The life-blood of rhymed translation is this—that a good poem shall not be turned into a bad one. The only true motive for putting poetry into a fresh language must be to endow a fresh nation, as far as possible, with one more possession of beauty. Poetry not being an exact science, literality of rendering is altogether secondary to this chief aim. I say literality, not fidelity, which is by no means the same thing. When literality can be combined with what is thus the primary condition of success, the translator is fortunate, and must strive his utmost to unite them; when such object can only be attacked by paraphrase, that is his only path.

Dante Gabriel Rossetti

Some years ago, when I first formed the notion of trying to translate a Swedish poet who wrote rhymed metrical verse, I asked Robert Bly—an experienced translator familiar with the Scandinavian literary scene—if he could recommend a few traditional poets to me. The first quotation given above is taken from his response (with his permission), and it puts a widely held view concisely. But I cannot endorse it. While obviously no poet "wants to see his meaning and images mangled," it's equally true that no traditional poet wants to see his songs mangled into something that can no longer be sung to the tune he set them to—watered down to free verse, in Richard Wilbur's happy phrase. The Rossetti quotation, serendipitously discovered in an anthology (*Twentieth Century Scandinavian Poetry*, edited by Martin S. Allwood, Oslo, 1950), is an indirect retort; the quote by Wilbur, taken from *Translation*, II (Winter, 1974), 7–8, is a direct and complete retort and the one I wish to countersign.

Reproducing Gullberg's poetry in English has been an exhausting and nerve-wringing business but also an enriching one. My efforts to follow the spirit of Rossetti's advice yet avoid the pitfalls warned against in Bly's letter have now and again resulted in compromise. *All* Gullberg's rhymes are exact; my occasional slant rhymes (bottom/autumn) and "cheat" rhymes (throughway/roué, wholesome/whole sum), and the two poems whose quatrains rhyme *abcd* instead of *abab*, represent compromises between music and meaning. Where choices had to be made I generally favored music in short lyrics, meaning otherwise. But I never compromised with form at all until I had examined every possibility I could invent for keeping to Gullberg's original metrical and rhyming schemes.

Most lines in the short lyrics and many in the terza rima poems are end-stopped in Gullberg's originals; some of these in my translations are not. On the other hand, I have very faithfully preserved his meters. I was forced to drop the feminine rhymes in the terzine—the most formally demanding poems I undertook to translate—and in "A Lake There Is," whose couplets alternate elegantly between masculine and feminine rhymes in the original. Feminine rhymes are more plentiful in Swedish than in English because so many definite articles are attached at the ends of nouns as single unaccented syllables, or as a single letter to a noun which already ends in an unaccented syllable (*bord* = table, *bordet* = the table; *dikt* = poem, *dikten* = the poem; *klocka* = clock, *klockan* = the clock), and the plural forms of nouns so often are made by adding an unaccented syllable to the singular noun, or a consonant with a vowel change (*dikter, klockor*). All definite nouns in the singular and many indefinite plural forms of nouns are potential feminine rhymes, and there are of course many other words which end with a single unaccented syllable.

This expedient aside, I took few liberties. One notable exception: "Singing Head," written originally in near-xxx/ Sapphics, unrhymed, of three five-stress lines followed by a two-stress line. I found this form impossible to retain without padding out the lines in English more than seemed acceptable. Two other points are also worth noting here. First, Gullberg's syntax is often tortuous; my syntactical convolutions fall far short of imitating the extremes he goes to in Swedish. Second, he habitually switches between present and past tense in the same narration. While there is no apparent reason for this vacillation, my early efforts to regularize the inconsistencies later seemed mistaken, and in these poems I have followed his erratic lead backwards and forwards in time.

The poems are arranged chronologically. In selecting the poems for the second part of the book I was guided about equally by personal preference and by the judgment of reliable critics as to which poems are essential and which expendable. I also very regretfully excluded a number of good and important poems because they proved so fiercely resistant to going into English undamaged. Before drawing up the final list I consulted four of the people who know Gullberg's work best: Dr. Ragnar Svanström, Swedish Academy Secretary Karl Ragnar Gierow, and Professors Carl Fehrman and Anders Palm of the *Litteraturvetenskapliga institutionen* at the University of Lund; both Gullberg experts, these last two were particularly helpful in suggesting important titles I might otherwise have overlooked.

BOOKS BY HJALMAR GULLBERG /xxxi

In an Unfamiliar City (*I en främmande stad*) 1927
Sonata (*Sonat*) 1929
Spiritual Exercises (*Andliga övningar*) 1932
Love in the Twentieth Century
  (*Kärlek i tjugonde seklet*) 1933
Gentleman, Single, Refined
  (*Ensamstående bildad herre*) 1935
To Overcome the World (*Att övervinna världen*) 1937
Five Loaves and Two Fishes
  (*Fem kornbröd och två fiskar*) 1942
Deathmask and Eden (*Dödsmask och lustgård*) 1952
Terzinas (*Terziner i okonstens tid*) 1958
Eyes, Lips (*Ögon, läppar*) 1959

Non-Occurring Thud

O nights the spirit spies through, lorn and lone!
The chasm has been bridged—but, ever since,
the other side's kept silent as a stone,
their herald testing not his instrument's
        tone!

Professor Urtstedt, brittle as a reed,
was once prevented thus from dropping off
by one who'd come from skoal and skirt to bed
in his apartment over the poor prof
        's head.

Just before twelve this gent, forgetting whose
unstable nerves his bedroom lay above,
took off and loudly tossed one of his shoes
onto the floor which was the ceiling of
        U's.

For the next shoe lay Urtstedt in the gloom
till daybreak waiting: but his neighbor's floor
was silent as the bottom of a tomb,
once the clock boomed its dozenth hollow-core
        boom.

No racket could have racked him like the non-
occurring thud did. Mr. Rake slept through
the night up there (in what condition one
may well imagine) with his other shoe
        on.

Inledning i frestelse

4/

Adjunkten Örtstedt rättar tyska stilar.
Då hoppar vid hans port ur ett par bilar
Das Ewig-Weibliche.

Ej dansar uppför trappan änglakören
ur Faust men små väninnor till vivören
Amandus Wikingson.

Det fnittras mycket ovanför adjunkten
som nästan är analfabet på punkten
Das Ewig-Weibliche.

Agent till yrket gör hans granne under:
han fångar kvinnor och förvärvar kunder
åt firman Wikingson.

Adjunkten nedanför, långt mindre talför,
är löjligt blyg (men ingalunda sval) för
Das Ewig-Weibliche.

I Örtstedts hjärta är ett sår upprivet.
Han frågar sig vem som får mest av livet,
han eller Wikingson.

Det smäller korkar och det dansas livligt.
En trappa upp drar honom obeskrivligt
Das Ewig-Weibliche.

Temptation

Professor Urtstedt's marking German papers.
Two cars stop at the door and from them capers
        Das Ewig-Weibliche.

No angel-choir from Faust pulled off the throughway
to waltz upstairs, but little pals of roué
        Amandus Vikingson.

Squeals overhead distract from quiz-correcting
our prof, a near-illiterate respecting
        Das Ewig-Weibliche.

His neighbor is a wonder-working he-man,
makes business boom by captivating women
        for his firm: Vikingson.

The prof, who can't be charming, is ignored by
and deathly shy of (though by no means bored by)
        Das Ewig-Weibliche.

In Urtstedt's heart is born a deep misgiving.
He asks himself who gets more out of living,
        he or Herr Vikingson.

Corks pop upstairs, they're dancing on his ceiling.
How keenly, indescribably appealing
        Das Ewig-Weibliche!

Till mosters minne

6/ För summan Örtstedt av en moster ärver
beslutar han att bota sina nerver.

Italiens solsken är det läkemedel
han ämnar köpa för sin stora sedel.

För hälsans vård blir han från skolan ledig.
I vårterminen far han till Venedig.

På vägen ska han från kupén se blåna
Romeos stad och Julias, Verona.

Emellertid är Östersjön förskräcklig.
Vid Rügen känner sig adjunkten bräcklig.

En tysk dam för till relingen den svage.
Han känner hennes arm kring bröst och mage.

Adjunkten Örtstedt tackar tusen gånger.
Hon svävar bort i matsal och salonger.

Arvtagarn kom ej längre än till Sassnitz.
I tullen ropar han bestört: Ich fass' nichts!

I bil försvunnen är den tyska flickan
med allt som innehölls i plånboksfickan.

Hans resehunger hade plötsligt mättats.
Men värre var att mostern förorättats.

Till dyster hemfärd räckte hans resurser.
Han återtog sin tjänst, gav sommarkurser.

Så länge brände honom samvetskvalet,
tills han fick hop det fulla kapitalet.

I skolans sparbanksbok står summan inne:
Adjunkten Örtstedts fond TILL MOSTERS MINNE.

Fund . . . In Fond Commemoration

With capital an auntie leaves him heir to,
Urtstedt decides to treat his nerves. Now: where to?

A warm Italian sunshine is the wholesome
medicament in which he'll sink the whole sum.

He takes a leave from teaching for his rest cure,
and sails for Venice in the spring semester.

En route he'll glimpse Verona, where still hovers
an aura of romance and star-crossed lovers.

A Baltic voyage, however, can be vastly
uncomfortable. At Rügen U. feels ghastly.

A German lady helps him to the railing.
He feels her arm round breast and stomach stealing.

A thousand thanks the grateful prof pronounces.
Away through lounge and dining room she flounces.

Heir Urtstedt got no farther than to Sassnitz.
At customs in dismay he cries: *Ich fass' nichts!*

The German girl has vanished God knows whither
and taken all his cash and papers with her.

His wanderlust had suddenly been sated.
Worse, auntie's memory'd been desecrated.

The sad trip home consumed his last resources.
He went to work again, gave summer courses.

A burning conscience drove him hell-for-leather
until he'd got the full amount together.

The school's books show the sum and this notation:
Fund, Urtstedt's Aunt, In Fond Commemoration.

Tinget i sig

En vinterafton läser Örtstedt Kant
och finner honom verkligt intressant.

Men filosofens tyska flyter tungt.
Snart somnar över boken vår adjunkt.

I nattens dröm gror dagens tankesådd.
Kant illustreras och blir lättförstådd.

Det kommer, svept i brokig omslagsfärg,
till Örtstedt ett paket från Königsberg.

Aktas för stötar! står det utanpå
med petig stil som verkar rokoko.

Avsändare och varans fabrikant
är ingen mindre än professor Kant.

Han granskar lådan vid sin fönsternisch.
Det står som innehåll: DAS DING AN SICH.

Kring tinget i sig själv, de vises sten,
är sinnevärlden blott ett brokigt sken.

Vem törs dock rycka undan slöjan kring
den rena verkligheten, tingens ting?

Adjunkten Örtstedt ryggar bort bestört
från det som ingen sett och ingen rört.

Om gåvan i hans grova händer sprack!
—Han returnerar den med tusen tack.

The Thing in Itself

Urtstedt reads Kant one winter eve and is
intrigued by certain principles of his.

But heavy flows the German of the sage,
and soon our prof is nodding o'er his page.

In dreams the seed of waking thought grows tall.
Kant isn't hard to understand at all.

A bright-wrapped package (here's the metaphor)
Arrives from Königsberg at Urtstedt's door.

"Fragile—Don't Drop!" in spidery letters, drawn
rococo-curlicued, appears thereon.

The sender, and the present's fabricant,
is no one lesser than Professor Kant.

He checks the label at his window-niche.
For "Contents" Kant put down DAS DING AN SICH.

Around this Thing the world we touch and see
is but a seeming, colored splendidly.

Who'd dare to rip the giftwrap and the strings
off pure Reality, the Thing of things?

Professor Urtstedt backs away unnerved
from what no hand has touched nor eye observed.

Think if his clumsy fingers let it crack!
With many thanks he mails the parcel back.

Bläckfisken

Trots allt fann adjunkten, att språkundervisning
var något man verkligen fängslades av.
Han gjorde en höst utan vidare spisning
en bläckfisk från södern till husdjur och slav.

En flink sekreterare har han sig skaffat,
fast svårt var att tukta en armstark polyp.
Hur ofta har Örtstedt ej bläckfisken straffat,
trots skollagens stadgar, med örfil och nyp!

Nu slipper han länge att slå och förmana:
på skrivbordet står i en vas hans elev,
som kan genom armarnas mångfald och vana
på en gång besvara ett åttatal brev.

Adjunkten har skaffat sig extrainkomster
tack vare sitt lärda och flitiga djur
som avsöndrar bläck till stilistiska blomster,
förtjust att få tjäna vårt språk, vår kultur.

The Octopus

In fact our professor found language-instruction
a thing for becoming enchanted withal.
One fall term he took without further production
an octopus home to be housepet and thrall.

A crack secretary, this muscular polyp,
though discipline proved problematic at first.
How often has Urtstedt with pinch and with wallop,
despite the school's rules, the unruly coerced!

Long since, he's dispensed with exhorting and caning;
a vase on his desk holds the pupil, no dunce,
which can through its multiple tentacles' training
efficiently answer eight letters at once.

A nice second income U. owes this artistic
assistant, a mollusk of powers and parts,
that squirts into flourishes grandly stylistic
its sepia, charmed with our language, our arts.

Det gamla trädet

Det gamla trädet blommar alla vårar.
Var pingst predikar det uppståndelsen
för Örtstedt som ej utan glädjetårar
betraktar sin från döden komne vän,
ett gammalt träd som blommor all vårar.

Så är all vänskaps art. Bland många tusen
har trädet av adjunkten blivit valt.
Hans egen arm var liksom bräckt och frusen,
då stormen brutit någon gren brutalt.
Så är all vänskaps art. En väljs bland tusen.

I orons dagar har hans själ haft nytta
av denna långa vänskap som ej brast.
Vad tröst för en person som brukar flytta,
att hans kamrat har rötter och står fast!
I orons dagar är ett träd till nytta.

The Old Tree

The old tree flowers each spring, an allegory
that preaches resurrection from the tomb
to Urtstedt, whose wet eyes behold the glory
of this his friend come back from death in bloom,
an old tree flowering for an allegory.

Such is the way of friendship. From ten thousand
this one tree was the tree that Urtstedt chose.
Whenever brutal storms broke off some bough's end
he felt as though his own arm cracked and froze.
Such is the way. One, chosen from ten thousand.

In troubled times his soul has found of service
this friendship never shattered, unsurpassed.
What comfort for a motile man so nervous
to have a rooted comrade who stands fast!
In troubled times a tree can be of service.

Söndagsfirande

En söndag trängas mellan träd och gårdar
familjefäder i moderna fordar.

Med manlig uppsyn sitter de vid ratten,
slätkammat folk som sover gott om natten.

Förbi kör Wikingson i chevroletten
med Tidström och två damer från baletten.

Allena ligger med sin smörgåspacke
adjunkten Örtstedt i en fjärran backe.

Där blommar marken som ett bibliskt Eden.
Och högt i träden ser han fågelreden.

Han vet ej skillnaden på korn och vete.
Han vilar efter veckans skolarbete.

En ringa del av det som gror och spirar,
på sjunde dagen Skaparen han firar.

Keeping the Sabbath

The roads through field and wood are jammed with hoards   /15
of Sunday drivers steering modern Fords.

With virile mien they view the passing sights,
sleek-headed men and such as sleep o' nights.

Among them Vikingson's new Chevy whirls
with Tidström and a brace of chorus girls.

Professor Urtstedt with his lunchsack lies
all by himself upon a distant rise.

The earth blooms like an Eden there. He sees
some birds' nests high above him in the trees.

He can't tell corn from wheat, this April fool.
He's resting from a week of work at school.

Of all that sprouts and buds one humble part,
he keeps the Sabbath Day with all his heart.

16/ Adjunkten Örtstedt skriver
vers för sin egen skull.
Då kommer detektiver
till grannen som är full.
Sin sista grogg förtärer
vivören Wikingson.
Han har gjort luftaffärer
och skrivit falska lån.

I Morgontuppen prålar
rubriken LUFTAFFÄRER.
Örtstedt sig darrhänt tvålar
och med sitt rakblad skär.
Djupt grannens kontroverser
med lagen honom rör.
Han samlar sina verser,
en lyrisk bankruttör.

Till kriminalpolisen
han skyndar samvetsöm.
« Ta mig! Här är bevisen.
Mitt liv var blott en dröm.
I alltför höga sfärer
förflöt min jordedag.
Vem har gjort luftaffärer,
Wikingson eller jag? »

Fraud

Urtstedt composes poems
for selfish pleasure's sake.
One day police detectives
collect that drunken rake.
His last of many highballs
swigs Vikingson the bawd.
He's passed bad checks and is to
be taken in for fraud.

The *Morning Cock's* huge headline
screams FRAUD from all the stands.
Professor Urtstedt washes
and shaves with trembling hands.
His neighbor's legal quarrels
have shocked him to the soul.
He bundles up his verses,
a lyrical bankroll.

Then rushes to the station
in guilt and penitence.
"My life's a dream. Arrest me!
Here, read the evidence.
My earthly day expired
in spheres too high to see.
By whom was fraud committed—
By Vikingson? or me?"

Återgång till
elementen

En åttaarmad bläckfisk står
med vaxljus i var hand.
Han lyfter vid adjunktens bår
sin kandelabers brand.

Var sak ska till sitt element
en gång bli återställd.
Hans trogne kontorist har bränt
vad Örtstedt skrev i eld.

På jorden var han arbetsträl
—jord ska han åter bli.
På sångens vingar steg hans själ
—i luften blev den fri.

Bläckfiskens chef i kistan sov.
Han släckte alla ljus.
En tonvåg sjöng i honom, dov
av undervattensbrus.

Han sköljde av sig vår kultur
i hamnens mörka bad.
Och åter var han vattendjur,
skrev aldrig mer en rad.

Return to
the Elements

Eight flames an octopus holds high,　　　　　
one in each hand, burn clear.
He lifts his candelabra by
Professor Urtstedt's bier.

Unto its element again
each thing shall be returned.
What Urtstedt wrote with blazing pen
his faithful clerk has burned.

On earth he was a drudge; ere long
earth he again shall be.
But high in air on wings of song
his soul went soaring, free.

The octopus his servant snuffed
the candles, one by one.
A wave-song pulsed in him and soughed
its muffled undertone.

He rinsed away our culture in
the harbor's murky brine
and was a water beast again—
nor wrote another line.

✝

En vän i handskar och med skjortan stärkt
bar hemligt ut adjunkten Örtstedts lik.
Det skedde helt och hållet obemärkt.
Vid porten fanns ej granris och musik.

Ej vältes nånsin ens en stol omkull
i Örtstedts våning som i andra mäns.
Mot husets folk var han så hänsynsfull,
att de har tvivlat på hans existens.

Det var i många ting en märklig man
som nu på okänd ort har funnit frid.
Av brist på framåtanda gjorde han
dock ingen större insats i vår tid.

Djärvt klyver laxen strömmen i en älv.
Adjunkten Örtstedt klöv ej livets ström.
Han levde blott i en för honom själv
fullständigt obekant kollegas dröm.

✝

A friend in gloves and starched shirtfront was sent
to take the body stealthily away.
This was a wholly unremarked event.
No mourning wreath adorned the door that day.

Since Urtstedt's conscience, stricter than most men's,
persuaded him that thoughtless noise was wrong,
the building's other, normal, residents
had doubted his existence all along.

And yet this man gone now to his reward
was quite extraordinary in his way.
For want of drive and forcefulness he scored
no more impressive tally in our day.

Fiercely a salmon fights the current's shove.
Urtstedt had never even learned to swim.
He only lived inside the fancy of
a colleague wholly unbeknownst to him.

SELECTED POEMS,
1937–1959

Sjön

Den helige herr Bernhard av Clairvaux
bjöd mig, sin väpnare, till stallet gå.

Hans konst att tiga är beundransvärd;
han nämnde inte målet för vår färd.

Vi red längs sjön som glänste spegelblank,
han böjd och grå, jag ung och mera slank.

Jag tänkte när vi ridit runtomkring:
min herres ärende var ingenting.

Jan tänkte tredje gång, vi red den runt:
min herre vet att friluftsliv är sunt.

Och sjunde gång, vid nådde klostrets mur:
min herre fröjdar sig åt Guds natur.

En lärka över oss sjöng vårens pris,
den tolfte gång vi red på samma vis.

Då bröts vår tystnad av min kommentar:
« Jag tycker också sjön är underbar!»

Så häpen kunde ej ett slag av spö
ha gjort mig som hans fråga: «Vilken sjö?»

Min herre hade ej lagt märke till
den spegelblanka sjön och lärkans drill.

Fast vi bevisligt gjorde samma tur,
red han på annat håll, jag vet ej hur.

Aldrig skall jag, hans väpnare, förstå
den helige herr Bernhard av Clairvaux.

The Lake

The holy knight Sir Bernard of Clairvaux
bade me, his squire, to the stable go.

My master keeps his council admirably;
he mentioned nothing of our goal to me.

Beside the glittering lake I rode with him,
he bowed and gray, I young erect and slim.

I thought when we had ridden round and back:
my master had no errand on the *lac*.

I thought when we had circled round it thrice:
my lord requires fresh air and exercise.

The seventh time we reached the cloister wall:
'tis Nature he refreshes him withal.

A lark above us sang a psalm to spring
the twelfth time we described the selfsame ring.

At that my comment broke our silence, thus:
"I also think the lake is marvelous!"

A lash's stroke unlooked-for could not make
my wits reel like his question then: "What lake?"

My master had not happened to remark
the mirror-shine of lake, the trill of lark.

We rode together; yet I do avow
he took some other road, I know not how.

And serve him knowing I shall never know
the holy knight Sir Bernard of Clairvaux.

26/

En konung som ej vet vartill han ämnas,
är född i natt av jordisk kvinnofamn.
Så helig är han, att han ej får nämnas.
Men fiskens bild är tecknet för hans namn.

Till djup som intet mänskoöga skådar,
sjönk jag i drömmens havsblå dykardräkt
för att berätta er vad ängeln bådar,
ni folk som med hans tecken är i släkt!

O hajstim som är sysselsatt vid fyren
med sönderstyckandet av sjömanslik,
tag tyst ur munnen sågtandsgarnityren
och kasta dem på bottnen av en vik!

O svärdfisk, lova mig att smida svärdet
till plog att plöja vattenfåror med!
Spjutrocka, skruva spjutet av och bär det
till sjön där all vapen läggas ned!

Jag bådar er en glädje utan like
bland bruna alger och bland röd korall.
Ty jord och hav skall ingå i det rike,
vars kung i natten föddes i ett stall.

Proclamation in the Sea

A king of woman's womb is born, too busy
with life tonight to know his life's design.
His name may not be named, so holy is he,
but draw a fish's picture for its sign.

In dream's deep-seablue diving suit subsiding
to depths no human eye has ever seen
I come to tell you of the angel's tiding,
you kinfolk to his symbol submarine.

O sharkpack by the point, with razor jawteeth
for haggling sailors' corpses washed ashore,
take softly from your mouths those sets of sawteeth
and let them settle on an inlet floor.

O swordfish, beat your sword into a plowshare
to plow blue water-furrows: promise me!
Spearfish, unscrew and stow away your browspear
where weapons all are laid down undersea!

Through reef and seaweed sounds my proclamation;
I tell you of incomparable joy.
For earth and sea shall come into the nation
whose king was born at midnight as a boy.

Liljorna på marken

En lilja tar ej tjänst och kan ej spinna,
och dock går ingen klädd som en av oss.
Du har oss prisat inför man och kvinna
som dagligen om bröd och kläder slåss.

Vi känna ej vad gråta är och skratta.
Att du blev gripen under handgemäng,
är ingenting som markens liljor fatta.
Vår uppgift är att dofta på en äng.

Från djurens värld av handling och av vilja
du lyfter din gestalt och gör den loss
och står i dag förvandlad till en lilja
på korsets stjälk och liknar en av oss.

The Lilies of the Field

A lily does not labor and spins nothing,
yet no one is arrayed like one of us.
To people squabbling over bread and clothing
you said a king was not more glorious.

We do not know what weeping is or laughter.
We cannot comprehend that soldiers beat
and mocked you, nor conceive of what comes after.
Our duty is to make a field smell sweet.

Now from the brutish world's self-willed consuming
we see you lift your shape and shake it loose
and stand transformed into a lily blooming
on cross's stalk, and look like one of us.

För vilsna fötter
sjunger gräset

För vilsna fötter sjunger gräset:
jag är din matta var du går
—räds ej, att natten förestår!
För vilsna fötter sjunger gräset:
mot hemmet styr jag dina spår.

För vilsna fötter sjunger gräset:
under mitt täcke sänks din bår
—räds ej, att natten förestår!
För vilsna fötter sjunger gräset:
du går mot hemmet var du går.

For Feet Astray
the Grass Is Singing

For feet astray the grass is singing:
"I am your carpet where you go—
fear not that darkness deepens so!"
For feet astray the grass is singing:
"I guide you homeward, swift or slow."

For feet astray the grass is singing:
"Over your grave my quilt shall grow—
fear not that darkness deepens so!"
For feet astray the grass is singing:
"You go still homeward where you go."

32/ Sjungande huvud som drev till sjöss med hårets
svarta segel hissat, med släckta ögon . . .
Ingen hand att röra det strida regnets
    harpsträngar, inga

kunniga fingrar kvar att beledsaga
denna odödliga stämma som blev slungad
från en thrakisk klippspets. Så berättar
sagan om Orfeus.

Honom slet vid pukors tumult i rökigt
fackelsken den larmande gudens kvinnor
sönder som en bock. När de rusigt sörplat
    i sig blodet,

slängdes till spis åt hundarna hans kön, åt
havet det ensamma huvudet som sjunger,
buret högt av vågorna mot sin fjärran
    hamnplats på Lesbos.

Löst från lemmarnas tyngd, från buken och dess
bihang kommer här den slutlige Orfeus:
stympad, blind, en havsmelodi för måsar
    —bara en spelmans

tvättade ansikte, bara en mun i sin na-
turliga infattning . . .

Singing Head

Singing head that drifted to sea with the black
sail of its hair set, with eyes extinguished . . .
No hand to touch the harpstrings of
    pelting rain, no

cunning fingers left to accompany
this immortal singing-voice hurled
from a Thracian crag. So the tale
    of Orpheus tells it.

To a rattle of kettledrums by smoky
torchlight the shrieking god's women tore him
to pieces like a he-goat. When they had
    slurped up his blood,

to the dogs was flung his sex, and to
the ocean the severed head that sings,
borne high by the waves toward its distant
    mooring on Lesbos.

Here, released from the weight of his limbs, from his
    belly and its
accessory, the ultimate Orpheus comes:
mutilated, blind, a chantey for seagulls
    —only the washed

face of a minstrel, only a mouth in its
natural setting . . .

34/

Med skygga fingertoppar trevar jag
över gudens ansikte, blundar
för att så mycken skönhet bländar,
men också av respekt. Budbärare,
i vilket tidevarv slets armen bort?
Var tappades hälarnas vingpar? När föll templet?
Där helig blygsel griper främlingen,
stiger med bruten glans din nakenhet
ur spillrorna. En gud är angelägen
om det passande avståndet till en dödlig.

Från hakan till det krusiga hårets hyacinter,
i en blindhet som gav rätten till beröring,
snuddade mina händer vid hans kind
av marmor, följde läpparnas kurva,
letande efter ordet som de slöt sig om.
Vad har vi för bevis på statyernas död
utom sönderfallet, avlägsenheten?
Vem vet hur länge de bor kvar i stenen?
Om de vill nå oss med ett sista budskap
måste vi möta dem på halva vägen.

Så for jag i min ungdom till Olympia
för att råka den av evighet utsände.
Med bistånd av de tio spejarna,
lätta som fjärilar, snabba
som ödlor bland ruiner, sporde jag den vackre
ledsagaren av skuggor vad hans mun
leende visste. Men i underjorden
förblev hans svar. Vad kunde mina händer?
Ensamma, ödsliga kommer mina händer
tillbaka. Deras kyla skrämmer mig.

With Timorous Fingertips
HERMES AT OLYMPIA

With timorous fingertips I fumble
across the god's face, shut my eyes
because so much beauty is blinding,
but also from respect. Tidings-bearer,
which epoch saw your arm torn away?
Where did your heels lose their wings? When did the temple
     fall?
Here where a shame of piety seizes the stranger
your nakedness rises in broken brilliance
from the rubble. A god is anxious
to keep his proper distance from a mortal.

From his chin to the hyacinths of his curly hair,
in a blindness that gave me the right to touch him,
my hands brushed the cheek
carved out of marble, followed the curve of the lips,
feeling for the word they closed upon.
What evidence have we that statues are dead
apart from their falling to pieces, their remoteness?
Who knows how long they go on living in the stone?
If they wish to reach us with a last message
we have to meet them halfway.

So in my youth I traveled to Olympia
to intercept eternity's messenger.
Assisted by ten scouts
light as butterflies, quick
as lizards among ruins, I besought that beautiful
companion of shadows for the knowledge
his smiling mouth concealed. But his answer
remained in the underworld. What could my hands
discover? Lonely, desolate, my hands
draw back. Their chill frightens me.

36/ Jag trodde på en gud men han visste det inte,
han fick aldrig veta att jag trodde på honom
ännu många år efter han var död.
Vid ingående förhör med mig om saken
blev jag upplyst om det verkliga förhållandet.
O slocknade stjärnors ljus som når försenat fram
till ögon i natten! Jag har skådat min gud
som han var i sin härlighet före katastrofen.
Han fick aldrig veta att jag trodde på honom
och att jag inte visste han var död.

I Believed in a God

I believed in a god but he didn't know it, /37
he was never to know that I went on believing in him
even after he'd been dead for years.
Questioning myself closely about this
brought the true state of affairs home to me.
O light of burnt-out stars belatedly reaching
eyes in the night! I have beheld my god
as he was in his splendor before the catastrophe.
He was never to know that I believed in him
and that I didn't know he was dead.

38/ Åt halvgudarna detta altare, dessa liljor,
åt halvgudarna som återstår att dyrka
efter gudarnas frånfälle som inte är en död
i vanlig bemärkelse men som vi här nere
inte kan uppfatta annat än som en död.

Mättade av ambrosia och nektar
nedlade de allsmäktiga sina tecken,
månskära, tjurhorn, spira. I stor avskildhet
bortom stjärnorna drog de sig tillbaka
ledda av honom som skiftar namn med ort,
konungen av de saliga höjderna.
Oförmögen att personligen hålla samman
det kosmiska skeendet lämnade han ifrån sig
blixtarna, de barnsliga leksakerna.
I orimligt ljus utplånad för vår syn,
längtande efter skapelsens glömska av skaparen
drog han bort med den klassiska gudavärlden.

I olikhet med de himmelska (som aldrig har levat
i vanlig bemärkelse) blev ni fostrade
som våra bröder, inte i den mening
ni sedan ville göra alla folk till bröder,
men för att hon som lagade vår mat
bevisligen hade fött oss. Redan då
kom underliga rykten i omlopp. Vi
dementerade i början rätt så handgripligt
den som bara sökte knysta nåt om mamma.
Man blev förstås fundersam längre fram
när ni började uppväcka lik och gå på vattnet.
Men också i fortsättningen

skulle ordningsmakten troligen ha blundat
var gång ni dräpte hydror och drev onda andar
i en svinhjord. Vad som bragte er på fall
var heller inte skrytet med er börd
men en renhet i uppsåtet—dessa ögon,

For the Demigods

For the demigods this altar, these lilies,
for the demigods left to worship
after that demise of the gods which is not a death
in the ordinary sense but which we here below
cannot comprehend except as a death.

Glutted on ambrosia and nectar
the almighty ones laid down their insignia:
sickle-moon, bull's horn, sceptre. They retired
into deep seclusion beyond the stars
led by him who changes name with location,
the king of the blessed heights.
Himself incapable of managing
the course of cosmic events, he put away
lightning bolts, his childish playthings.
Blanched from our sight in a brightness beyond belief
longing for his creatures to forget their creator
he drew back, and the classical god-world with him.

Unlike those heavenly ones (who have never lived
in the ordinary sense) you were brought up
as our brothers, not the way
you later wished to change everyone into brothers,
but because she who prepared our food
unquestionably had borne us. Even then
strange rumors were starting to circulate. At first
we used to rough up anyone who even tried
insinuating things about Mamma.
Naturally we grew thoughful later on
when you began to raise the dead and walk on water.
But even after that

the authorities probably would have looked the other way
whenever you slew Hydras and drove unclean spirits
into a herd of swine. What brought about your downfall
wasn't boasting about your ancestry, either,
but a purity of purpose—those eyes,

dessa ord och händer! Man stod inte ut!
Vi medger villigt att de tolv storverken
utfördes till belåtenhet, att stall
och helgedom behöver rensas. Men
bedrifternas baksida, blodsoffren, stanken
och den ångest som är halvgudens modersarv
har hjältesagan dolt för eftervärlden.

Det utmärkande för halvgudarna är deras godhet
och våldsamma död. Aldrig sattes bödlarnas
kunskap och tålamod på större prov.
Om du såg en bläckfisk på en sydländsk kaj
bli slagen i stenläggningen som hade den ett dussin liv
i varje arm: lika segslitna är halvgudarna
i en plågokammare, på en avrättningsplats
—det är faderns heliga säd som förlänger lidandet.
Ett dunkelt minne av odödlighet
sitter kvar i den blodiga massan. Därför
är det ofta så arbetsamt att hudflänga,
stycka och bränna deras kött.

Åt er dessa liljor, dessa isopsstänglar,
åt er detta altare som inte är ett altare
i vanlig bemärkelse men en trappa av sång
till de outhärdliga
hjälparna i vår nöd.

those words and hands! People couldn't stand that!
We concede willingly that the twelve labors
were performed to satisfaction, that stable
and temple need to be cleansed. But
the heroic saga has concealed from posterity
the backside of these deeds, the blood-sacrifices, the stench,
and the anguish a demigod's mother bequeaths to him.

Demigods are marked out by their goodness
and violent deaths. Never were executioners'
cunning and patience put more severely to the test.
If you've ever seen an octopus on a southern quay
hurled upon the stone paving as though it had a dozen lives
in every arm: the demigods are equally durable
in a torture-chamber, at a place of execution—
their father's divine seed prolongs their suffering.
A dim memory of immortality
sits tight in the bloody mass. This explains why
it is often so arduous to flay them,
to disjoint and burn their flesh.

For you these lilies, these stalks of hyssop
for you this altar which is not an altar
in the ordinary sense but a staircase of song
            to the unendurable
            helpers at our need.

Det finns en sjö
och sedan aldrig mer

Det finns en sjö och sedan aldrig mer,
och floden slätas ut i den grå spegeln
som ingen strand inramar, inga roddarslag
ska spräcka. O ni saligt bortvända, ni döda,
i självtillräcklig skönhet vilande!
Gudarnas avund rubbar ej er frid. Vad annat
än en förlängning av mandatet är
den skröpliga evärdlighet de har förunnats?

Om gamars närhet skvallrar fågelspillning.
Att lösa oss från rums- och tidsurskillning
har ljudlöst vita klockor ringt för oss
på dessa ängar av asfodelos.
Vår skepnad är till synes bibehållen;
blott puls och andning lämnas i kontrollen
och skuggan av mig själv blir släppt förbi,
ett håltomt eko av en melodi,
en sista rossling ur ett sängomhänge.
Vår död är ofullgången än sålänge.
Ty dessa ängar utan fågelsång
är blott en anhalt och en övergång.
Oss förde färjan bara från den ena
overkligheten, åldringar och spena-
barn, till den andra, lite längre bort,
utvandrare i väntan på transport.
Där porten sluter sig och hunden skäller,
regerar tvillingparet Varken-Eller,
lydfurstar i ett gränsland. Ingen vet
vad man och kvinna har för olikhet,
när skiljemur på skiljemur ger vika:
gammal och ung,
                        tiggare, kung,
                                        kvittar lika.
Så faller svepningar och ornament,
alltmedan hunden stirrar oavvänt

A Lake There Is
and Ever Nothing Then

A lake there is and ever nothing then,
and the river is smoothed out in the gray mirror
which no strand frames, no oar-strokes
will ever crack. O ye blessedly averted ones, ye dead
in self-sufficient beauty resting!
The envy of the gods disturbs not your peace. What
but a lengthening of their mandate is
the frail eternity they have been granted?

Birddroppings gossip of the vultures near.
To loose us from our sense of When and Where
white little bells all soundlessly have pealed
for us on this narcissus-quilted field.
Our shape appears to be kept back at death;
the checkpoint confiscates but pulse and breath
and slips the shadow through that once was me,
a hollow echo of a melody,
a final rattle from a curtained bed.
Thus far, we still are incompletely dead.
Because this field where songbirds never come
is just a stop, a place to transfer from.
The ferry only brought us, elderly
and infants, from one non-reality
into the next, a little more remote,
emigrants who are waiting for the boat.
Two vassal princes of a borderland—
the pair of twins called Neither-Nor—command
where the dog whimpers and the portals close.
How man and woman differ no one knows
with barrier on barrier undone:
old and young,
                beggarman, king,
                        equal one.
So while the shrouds and trappings of the dead
fall from us, the dog's stare stays riveted

på jordiskt liv som är tilländalupet.
Och floden vaggar oss mot spegeldjupet
som i gestaltlös vila återger
Narkissos död och sedan aldrig mer.

on earthly life's conclusion. And the stream
cradles us toward the mirrordeeps agleam
which reproduce in formless rest therein
Narcissus dead, and ever nothing then.

På Lemnhults kyrkogård
1804-1875

46/   Här vilar bonden Johan Magnusson
som byggde tjugotre orgelverk i Växjö stift.
Tidigare fann han sin bästa ro vid kvarnforsen
i en sommarkväll. Han prisade naturen
på rimmad vers, en anspråkslös elev
till Herr Biskopen. Han kunde också riva färg
och på underdånig framställning från denna församling
fick han kunglig medalj för sitt tavelmåleri.
Han hade lärt av Hörberg och vännen Marcus Larsson,
de sjungande forsarnas ojämförlige avbildare,
och många håller före att i Skirö kyrka
hans flyttade altartavla vida överträffar
den nya som målades av kyrkoherdens fru.

Födda till dagsverken i skog och mark,
en bondes händer—varför blev de valda?
Vem utrannsakar varför de blev valda?
När tonen från himlen behövde nya redskap
för att klinga renare och högre i Småland
gavs uppdraget åt denne Johan Magnusson.
Det är han som har uppfunnit psalmpositivet
på vilket en mångfald kristna melodier
kunde vevas i skolorna till barnens fromma,
och vart år vid Sigfridsmässan på Växjö torg
stod en dräng och sålde hans speldosor.
Men på höjden av sin mandom, fyrtiotvå år gammal,
var den självlärde färdig med det större instrument
om vilket han, en diktare, brukat yttra:
Orgeln kan säga till hjärtat vad ord ej förmå.—
Och Johann Sebastian Bach höll sitt intåg i Kråksmåla.

Här i Lemnhult byggde han det sista verket.
Anonyma insändare i tidningen Triaden
hade uppfordrat skomakaren att förbli vid sin läst;
men det ord passar förvisso bättre på en orgelbyggare

In Lemnhult Churchyard
1804–1875

Here lies farmer Johan Magnusson,
who built twenty-three organs in Växjö diocese.
In youth he found his best repose at the mill-rush
of a summer night. He praised Nature
in rhyming verse, an unpretentious student
of my lord Bishop. He knew also the art of grinding pigments,
and upon humble petition from this parish
received a royal medal for his picture painting.
He had learned something from Hörberg and his friend
      Marcus Larsson,
incomparable portrayer of singing waterfalls,
and many are of the opinion that in Skirö Church
his altarpiece, now removed, is far superior
to the new one painted by the pastor's wife.

Born to day labor in forest and field,
a farmer's hands—why were they chosen?
Who can fathom why they should have been chosen?
When heavenly music required new instruments
that it might ring out more purely and loudly in Småland
the commission was awarded to this Johan Magnusson.
He it was who invented the hand-organ
on which a variety of Christian psalms
could be cranked out in the schools for the children's benefit;
and every year at the Sigfrid Market in Växjö Square
a farmhand stood, hawking his music-boxes.
But in the prime of his manhood, forty-two years old,
this self-taught artist completed the greater instrument
about which he, a poet, used to say:
The organ can speak to the heart as words cannot.—
And Johann Sebastian Bach made his grand entrance in
      Kråksmåla.

He built his last organ here in Lemnhult.
Anonymous correspondents to the newspaper *Triaden*
had admonished the shoemaker to stick to his last,
but the proverb which says that the work praises the master

som säger att verket prisar mästaren.
Under arbetets gång förbättrade leverantören
med sinnrika påfund sina skapelser,
och Domkyrkoorganisten skrev vid en besiktning
att konsten i hans hand var mera än levnadsyrke.
Så ofta husbonden uppe i hantverksrummet
intonerade Fugara, Principal, Fleut d'amour,
måste allt arbete läggas ner på gården Nässja
—ingenting fick störa utom forsen som sjöng.
I längden var det inte bra för lantbruket.
Den som bygger en orgel åt Gud
låter sin gård förfalla.

I främmande stift
fann den mångkunnige bondens ättlingar sin utkomst.
Av hans orgelverk finns några i behåll
efter hundra år. Ett spelar i mig.

surely suits an organ-builder better.
During construction, the artist
improved his creations with ingenious ideas,
and the Cathedral organist wrote after an inspection
that the skill in his hand was more than professional.
Whenever the master up in his workshop
was voicing *Fugara; Principal, Fleut d'amour,*
work had to stop completely on Nässja Farm—
no disturbance was permitted save the waterfall's singing.
In the long run, that wasn't good for farming.
He who builds an organ to God
lets his land fall fallow.

In unfamiliar dioceses
this versatile farmer's descendants found their livelihood.
Some of his organs still survive
after a hundred years. One plays in me.

Delos, ett ode
till de unga

Jag såg Apollons födelseplats. Hans skepp
av sten och de arkaiska lejonens
        livvakt såg en turist på out-
härdliga ljushav. I systerns båge

är strängen som ger döden, men han fick sju
att ordna versens turer och fötternas
        i växeldansen kring den sköna
ordningens sköne korag, öns herre . . .

Kollega med en blomma i munnen, hör
en sanning: medelåldern har ingen sång.
        Erfarenhet—visst, utmärk! Men den
gudarna älskar dör ung. Jag önskar

därnäst dig överleva din starkhet och
dig själv och finna, blottad på allt—som jag
        fann ön (ty oundvikligt är vårt
skeppsbrott) där tigandet sjöng—ditt Delos.

Delos, an Ode
to the Young

I saw Apollo's birthplace. His ship of stone
and bodyguard of archaic lions saw
      a tourist on unendurable oceans
   of light. In his sister's bow

is the string that renders death, but he had seven
to order the turns of verse and of feet in the changing
      dance about the lord of the island, fair
   choragus of that fair ordering . . .

Colleague with the flower in your mouth, attend
a truth: middle age has no song.
         Experience—certainly, excellent! But
   him the gods love dies young. I wish

you otherwise to outlive your strength
and your time and find, bereft of everything—
      as I found the island (for unavoidable is
   our shipwreck) where the silence sang—your Delos.

52/ Som när i sin bedövande butik
urmakarn lyssnar klockan tolv till slagen
—den ena takten ej den andra lik,

och även göken låter nyuppdragen—
var skogen fullhängd med så mycken sång
att kvinnan stod förvirrad och betagen.

Ranunkelgul, en tappad medaljong,
för hennes fot låg tjärnen. En hop spillning
upplyste om var rådjur haft sin gång.

Flöjtande, pip, en trasts bel canto, drillning,
lövsångarvisans folkton, allt, moll, dur,
på en gång, utan paus och tidsurskillning,

framfördes efter något partitur
som kvinnan kände att hon skulle ösa
en hemlig insikt, en förhoppning ur,

om hon fick samband med det meningslösa
utbrottet av musik. Om strupen vred
sig plötsligt hennes händer i nervösa

rörelser tills en rossling gav besked
att krampen var förbi. Hon kände varken
sorg eller glädje längre. Hon sjöng med.

En kvinna sjöng och stjärnblom täckte marken . . .

Stellaria

As when the old clockmaker's clocks all strike
together, and he listens to them sound
the deafening stroke of twelve—no two in like

time, and the cuckoo too has just been wound—
the woods were hung so full of so much song
the woman stood bewildered and spellbound.

Buttercup-gold, a locket or a gong,
the tarn lay at her foot. A little heap
of droppings showed where deer had passed along.

All: trill, flute, thrush's pure bel canto, cheep,
wood warbler's folktune, major, minor, more,
at once, no rests and no attempt to keep

time, were performed according to a score
from which the woman felt she might express
a hope, an insight hidden theretofore,

could she but tune in on the meaningless
outbreak of music. Round her slim throat flew
her hands in sudden flights of nervousness,

wringing until a rattle came, the cue
her cramp was over. She felt neither mirth
nor sorrow any longer. She sang too.

A woman sang and starwort cloaked the earth . . .

Häger på bryggan

Jag låg på bryggan naken då en häger
stod ljudlöst, kommen som från ingenstans,
bakom och lät mig på mitt hårda läger

död som en sten bli kvar i solens glans.
Landskapet hade fått en annan mening.
Jag ägde inte bryggan. Det var hans.

Jag var en kvarglömd rest, en förorening.
Hans tid var inne där han stod på vakt—
min var ett vakuum, en tågförsening,

bortfall av syfte i en passiv akt.
Den sky som bar min dröm för vita segel
gick plötsligt i det blå med annan frakt,

och sjön jag hållit som min runda spegel
på bryggans skaft var lössgjord från min sjö.
Det sus som gick i vassen kom var regel

från förr att skälva utan kraft, ett rö.
Var det en fantasibild som blev kluven,
eller en verklighet som skulle dö?

En värld gick mig ur händerna. Var tjuven
den grå staty som till min sträckbänk kom
och utan avsikt långsamt drog åt skruven?

När hägern lyfte lika ljudlöst som
han stod på bryggan utan varning, hävde
jag mig på axlarna och såg mig om.

Förlamningen var borta och den kvävde
insöp en luft som återfick sin glans.
Var det sitt rike som den andre krävde?

Finns det en ordning bortom människans?
Ett tryck vek från mitt hjärta, en förhårdning.
Tre dar kom hägern så. Jag såg i hans.

ankomst ett varsel om en sådan ordning.

Heron on the Dock

I lay sunbathing naked on the dock
when back of me a silent heron stood,
come out of nowhere, letting me stay stock-

still in the sunshine on my cot of wood.
The landscape changed its meaning in a flash.
This was his dock, not mine. I understood:

I was just dirt, a pile of castoff trash.
His time had come, mine turned into a jest—
a train-delay—a vacuum—balderdash—

collapse of purpose in a passive *geste*.
The cloud that set my dream for canvas sailed
away with other cargo, bearing west,

and the round lake, a looking-glass I'd held
by the dock's handle, loosened from my lake.
The rushes rustled and the old rules failed,

rendered as frail as reeds, as like to shake.
Was what I'd seen a truth no longer true,
or had a vision been exposed as fake?

A world I'd curled my fingers round slipped through.
Had that gray statue stolen it, who'd found
my rack and, not on purpose, turned the screw?

The heron flapped aloft with neither sound
nor warning, as he'd come; then I could dare
to heave my shoulders up and look around.

Paralysis was over and the air
I drank restored to brightness and to ease.
Was it his realm the other claimed? Is there

some ordering beyond humanity's?
A pressure left my heart, a callous thing.
Three days the heron came. I saw in these

comings a sign of such an ordering.

Insnöad

Insnöad under stjärnor, efter stormen,
står jag och kramar stjärnor i min vante
till en klump is som ödelägger formen.

Här följde jag i juli den galante
råbockens kärleksstig och småsjöng mina
terziner. Den må applådera Dante

som fann behag i lånet från Divina
Commedia och anar orgelbruset
från stjärnor som en sångare såg skina.

Min badviks vatten ligger bottenfruset.
Radion fyller med sin nyårsklocka
den tända salen i det vita huset,

där jag ser husfrun sväva som en docka
tyst i ett scenrum för marionetter.
Men vilka är de toner jag vill locka

från himlen? Vilken tröst för oförrätter
kan en gudomlig komedi bereda?
Var fanns om ej i dessa ljusa nätter

som gjorde sina Vintergator breda,
en hög geometri, en hemlig stadga?
Från år av olust kommer jag, av leda

och vanmakt i en värld som tuggar fradga.
Vad visste jag om form som kan förlösa?
Vad visste jag om vårt behov av stadga?

För den som av det slappa och porösa
fått nog blev stjärnor tända dubbelt klara.
En källa finns för alla som vill ösa.

Är mänskligheten dömd? Om sådan fara
är i sin oskuld sången omedveten.
Triangel länkas till triangel bara

och Linjen löper ut i evigheten . . .

Snowbound

Snowbound by starlight after the long storm
I stand and squeeze stars tightly in my glove
into a lump of ice, destroying form.

I traced the gallant roebuck's path of love
last summer, softly singing verse of mine,
terzinas. Let them clap for Dante who've

rejoiced to borrow thus from his divine
Commedia, and divined an organ's cry
from stars that showed a singer how they shine.

My swimming-cove lies frozen through. Nearby
the radio fills up the lighted hall
of the white house with New Year's bells, and I

can see the housewife floating like a doll
silently on the window's puppet stage.
What kind of music do I wish to call

from heaven? How can comedy assuage
injustices, divine or not? And where,
if not in these light nights that set the gauge

to build their Milky Ways so broad, was there
a stable strength, a high geometry?
I come from years of loathing, of despair

and impotence; the world's mouth froths at me.
How could I know of form as saving grace?
How could I know we crave stability?

The stars were kindled doubly clear in space
for one fed up with flab and sponginess.
For all who thirst, there is a watering-place.

Is mankind doomed? Song in its simpleness
finds such a danger easy to ignore.
Triangle's linked but to triangle—yes,

and Line runs out and out forevermore . . .

Skrivet på en födelsedag
av poeten till sig själv

Det bästa är att aldrig vara född.
Av ingen olyckskorp och kverulant
är ordet sagt, av ingen övergödd

vällusting när han, slagen till en slant,
betalar notan och i svart kaross
blir hämtad. Jag citerar en bekant

körsång ur Oidipus på Kolonos.
Mer oförstört än templets marmorfris
är ordet som från scenen nådde oss.

En man som i sin ålders höst vann pris,
en diktare på väg från livets fest,
en vis man säger vad en annan vis

sagt före honom: aldrig född är bäst.
Är detta sanningen vem kommer då
det bästa närmast? En belevad gäst

som vet när han ska säga tack och gå.

Written on the Poet's
Birthday to Himself

What's best for man is never to be born.
No stormy-petrel malcontent said this,
no drunk *gourmand* with heartburn, feeling worn

and sick, while settling up, for emphasis,
before the hearse arrives for him and he's
been hauled away. No, what I'm quoting is

a famous chorus speech from Sophocles
come down to us, this proverb from the stage,
less time-wrecked than the temple's marble frieze.

A man praised in the autumn of his age
who left the party at its liveliest,
a poet-sage, says what another sage

said long before he did: that it were best
not to be born at all. This being so,
who does the next-best thing? A courteous guest

who knows when he should say his thanks and go.

Tag bort fotografierna

Tag bort fotografierna! Vi döda
är känsliga för dylikt första tiden.
Anpassningen sker inte utan möda
till friden över allt förstånd, till friden

som ni har unnat oss i dödsannonsen.
Släpp oss! Er sorg förlänger vår begravning.
Namn och profil i marmorn och i bronsen
när vi ska byta form och ändra stavning,

är hinder som vi hellre vore utan.
I natt är vi den snö som faller flinga
vid flinga ljudlöst. Ansikte mot rutan,
vems namn är det du ropar? Vi har inga.

Put the Photographs Away

Oh, put the photographs away! This first while
we dead are sensitive, such things demanding.
Not without effort do we trade our erstwhile
concerns for peace that passeth understanding,

the peace of the obituary pages.
Let go! Your grief releases us too slowly.
Name and profile unaltered down the ages
in bronze and stone, when we shall alter wholly,

but hinder us. We are the silent-falling
indifferent snow which settles flake by aimless
soft flake tonight. Whose name is that you're calling,
face pressed against the window? We are nameless.

62/ Jag trodde månen var en gul ballong
som rika farbröder från Österlanden
gav Jesusbarnet under änglasång.

Vid hemligt snöre höll han den i handen;
att inte släppa det kom han ihåg.
Där i sin prakt den stod vid himlaranden

fanns Betlehem och stallet där han låg.
Steg den i vanlig storlek över taken
var flykten till Egypten vad man såg.

Men dit var långt och jag var aldrig vaken
när den var framme och togs in. Jag fick
själv en ballong och när jag tänkt på saken,

beslöt jag i ett givmilt ögonblick
att Jesusbarnet genast skulle få den
och månen ha ett sällskap där han gick.

Min stad var rik på gröna parkområden
och med familjen satt jag på en bänk.
En stjärna tändes och jag släppte tråden

och tyckte att nu brast en jordisk länk.
Ballongen steg och stjärnan brann för sonen
i skyn—men ingen tog emot min skänk.

Och det fanns ingen måne utom månen.

Balloons

I thought the moon a helium balloon
the Wise Men gave to Jesus on that cold
first Christmas while the angels sang their tune

called Gloria. He did as he was told.
He had a secret string to hold it by.
It hung at the horizon, huge and gold,

to show where Bethlehem and stable lie.
It sailed moon-size above the roofs a way
tracing the flight to Egypt through the sky.

But that was far, and I could never stay
awake till it was taken in, to see.
I got a big balloon myself one day,

and in a burst of generosity
decided I would give the infant king
mine, and the moon a bit of company.

My family liked parks. That evening
we all sat on a bench in one, and when
a star came out, and I let go the string,

I felt an earthly link snap there and then.
The star burned for the son, and my balloon
sailed up—but no one ever took it in.

And there was still no moon except the moon.

Bara en önskan

Bara en önskan, bara en.
Ligger och ber och tigger
så det borde röra en sten.
Men också stenen ligger.

Henne jag slutligen dröjde hos
håller jag, handen, rösten.
Som när vi fann en försenad ros,
praktfull, unik, i hösten;

efter en frostnatt var sagan all,
rosen låg utströdd bara.
Vissnande aldrig. Ett sönderfall.
Slut. —Så skulle det vara.

Djupare in, genom märg och ben,
dagar och nätter långa:
bara en önskan, bara en.
Somliga har så många.

Only One Wish

Only one wish, one wish alone—
lie here and plead and call so
you might swear it could move a stone.
But here the stone lies also.

Holding her, hand and voice, repose
washes me top to bottom.
As when we found a belated rose,
splendid, unique, in autumn:

after a frostnight the rose lay dead,
scattered as wide as *could* be.
Fallen to pieces. Would never fade.
Finished. —That's how it should be.

Deeper within, through marrow and bone,
nights upon noondays rounding,
only one wish, one wish alone.
Others' keep on compounding.

Jag bor vid ett rastställe

Jag bor vid ett rastställe, långsmalt, havsomflutet
en utsträckt hand av vildros och susande gräs
som öppnar eller knyter sig. Här är slutet
på kartan över landet, ett yttersta näs.

Ett rastställe också för människan att bada
och bo vid men anlagt för högre bruk än så.
Ty över mitt huvud är byggd en autostrada,
en resväg till södern, den äldsta i det blå.

De höstliga fågelsträckens väg, om våren
den eviga återkomstens. Nedåtvänd
är rastställets båge som rör vid rosensnåren,
av häger och kungsfågel i en urtid spänd.

En strandremsa bara med det låga gräset
som fåglarna valde på sin pilgrimsgång.
Jag bor under vägen som går till paradiset.
O, leva i ett vingbrus och dö i en sång!

I Dwell at a Resting-Place

I dwell at a resting-place—long, narrow, sea-encircled—
of wild rose and rustling grasses, an outstretched hand
which opens or clenches itself. The map of the country
stops here, upon this outermost jut of land.

A resting-place where people can settle also
and swim at, but meant for loftier purpose too.
For over my head is built a superhighway,
a southbound road, the oldest one in the blue.

The flyway of autumn migrants, and in springtime
the way of eternal return. Its curving bow
bent here in an ancient year by heron and kingbird
swoops down and touches the wild rose thicket below.

A stretch of strand with the short grass only, chosen
by birds on pilgrimage as they fly along.
My house lies under the road that points toward heaven.
Oh, to live in a wingrush and die in a song!

68/
Om kärleken och döden
finns det sägner utan tal;
men hennes som ur gravens mull
blev förd till kungens sal,
har gjort kärleken och döden
till ett i Portugal.
Den döda drottningen.

Det var Inès de Castro,
det var Pedro och hans brud.
Han tog rosen från Kastilien
till maka inför Gud,
och han såg sin ros bli skövlad
på den gamle kungens bud.
Den döda drottningen.

Hans ord föll: «Kan jag gråta
vid min faders grift med fog?
För att han dräpt mitt hjärtas dam
har jag fällt tårar nog.»
Hans ord: «Nu är jag konung
och drottning hon som dog.»
Den döda drottningen.

Det var Inès de Castro.
Hon blev förd i procession;
folk stod med tända vaxljus.
Vid kröningsklockans ton
blev hon förd till Alcobaça
och uppsatt på en tron.
Den döda drottningen.

Med krona på sitt huvud,
svept i brokad och band
blev hon av hovets riddare
och damer kysst på hand.
Hon satt vid kungens sida
och hans land var hennes land.
Den döda drottningen.

Ballad

Legends of love and death abound,
we cannot count them all;
but hers who out of graveyard mold
was borne to palace hall
has linked together love and death
for aye in Portugal.
  The late belovéd Queen.

She was Inès de Castro,
she was Pedro's own adored.
He took this pure Castilian rose
to wife before the Lord,
and he saw his rose be ravaged
at the King his father's word.
  The late belovéd Queen.

He spake thus: "Have I cause to weep
my father's crypt beside?
I have ere this shed tears enough
for that he slew my bride."
He spake: "But I am King now
and she is Queen that died."
  The late belovéd Queen.

She was Inès de Castro.
A procession bore her round;
folk stood with lighted candles.
To churchbells' joyous sound
she was brought to Alcobaça
set on her throne and crowned.
  The late belovéd Queen.

With crown on head, appareled
in brocade and broidered band,
the knights and ladies of the Court
came forth to kiss her hand.
She sat beside His Majesty
and his land was her land.
  The late belovéd Queen.

Hans ord: « Det är min vilja
att min gemål och jag
med fötterna mot varandra,
sarkofag mot sarkofag,
ska vila hos varandra
ända till domedag. »
  Den döda drottningen.

« När uppståndelsens basuner
hörs skalla ur det blå,
ska vi resa oss mot varandra
och genast upprätt stå
ansikte mot ansikte;
och vad kan döden då? »
  Den levande drottningen.

He spake thus: "I desire
that my consort and her groom
with feet against each other's,
my tomb against her tomb,
shall rest beside each other
until the Day of Doom."
    The late belovéd Queen.

When the trump's blast from heaven
gathers the faithful in,
we shall rise toward one another
and upright stand, amen!
my face against the Queen's face;
and what can Death do then?"
    The living belovéd Queen.